In a distant land, far, far away,
is a little town called Backwards Bay.

The folks who live in Backwards Bay
say "Goodnight" to start the day!

They put on their clothing the opposite way.

A big turkey dinner's the first meal of the day!

4

People heat up their water in an ice-cube tray!

They comment, "Nice weather!"
when it's raining and gray.

 6

They hold their umbrellas
to catch all the spray!

7

School doesn't begin until after kids play!

The school bus backs up,
and they're on their way!

During class, the teacher asks,
"Who's teaching today?"

And every day but ONE is your birthday!

In the evening, folks have breakfast,
and after that they say—

"Rise and shine! Good morning!
See you yesterday!"

Listen to the riddle sentences. Add the right letter or letters to the -ay sound to finish each one.

1  The opposite of night is ___ay.

2  When horses are hungry, you can feed them ___ay.

3  The month that comes before June is ___ay.

4  To make a dog sit still you tell it to ___ay.

5  In art class, I formed a bowl out of ___ay.

**6**   My aunt and uncle live far ____ay.

**7**   I am lost, can you show me the ___ay?

**8**   It is easier to carry food and drinks
on a ____ay.

**9**   Look! The boat is sailing into the ___ay.

**10**   When you mix black and white,
it makes ____ay.

Now make up some new riddle sentences using - ay

# -ay Cheer

Give a great holler, a cheer, a yell

For all of the words that we can spell

With an A and a Y that make the sound –ay,

You'll find it in hay and way and May.

Two little letters, that's all that we need

To make a whole family of words to read!

Make a list of other –ay words. Then use them in the cheer!